A Journey through

Gloucestershire

An anthology of pictures and poetry

John & Sally Ryde

Historic Gloucester Docks.

First published in Great Britain in 2007 by;
Centenary Arts Ltd
19 Walnut Close, Cheltenham, Gloucestershire, GL52 3AF
01242 518 561
www.centenaryarts.com

Designed by Pritchards Creative Communications,
Gratton House, Gratton Street, Cheltenham, GL50 2AS.
01242 226 316
www.pritchardscreative.co.uk

Illustrations by Maltings Partnership
www.maltingspartnership.com

ISBN 978-0-9556195-0-2

Pitville Pump Rooms, Cheltenham.

INTRODUCTION

What is Poetry? How's that for a cliché to start? The OED's answer is "literary composition that is given intensity by particular attention to diction (sometimes involving rhyme), rhythm, and imagery." A good example of definition by committee.

My answer is that poetry is the purest of all art. It is music without notes, painting without pictures, literature without facts.

Poetry is the conscious dream. It happens only inside the creator's head and the written word is an attempt to convey that dream to others. We have added photographs to try and aid this process.

The book is a celebration of Gloucestershire but on a couple of occasions Sally, in search of the best picture, wandered into the adjoining county. The shot of the Evenlode was taken just over the Oxfordshire border and Tintern Abbey stands on the Monmouth bank of the Wye.

Many of the poets have a Gloucestershire connection, although at times obscure. Tennyson had a house in Cheltenham, Byron was a frequent visitor to the town, Morris lived in Kelmscott, Masefield and Elizabeth Browning were born just over the border to the west and Shakespeare to the north. As well as the famous sons of the County, Gurney, Harvey, Lee et al, there were the Dymock Poets, an extraordinary collection of talent that gathered for a few years in the village and wrote some of their best poetry. I have no excuse for including Seamus Heaney or William Butler Yeats save that no anthology of poetry could possibly be complete without them.

I have collected the poems during my life and kept them in a battered manila folder for use when solace is needed. The photographs are all taken by my daughter Sally who does this sort of thing for a living. We are both Cheltenham folk and a year ago we thought we knew everything there was to know about Gloucestershire, and each other. We were wrong!

The Severn from Pope's Hill in the Forest of Dean.

Much loved Forest of Dean poet and writer who died in 1981.

From this
NIGHT
the
STARS...

HOW CAN this ever pass away,
This home of hills and trees?
I rather think on Judgement Day,
When all are on their knees,
They'll find who through the clouds shall rise
That Gloucestershire is Paradise,
And Heaven's fields are these.

Leonard Clark

A poppy field near Sevenhampton.

James Stephens was born in Dublin in 1882. It must be very difficult to become a great Irish Poet, there is so much competition, but his voice was unique.

In the Poppy *field*

...MAD Patsy said, he said to me,

That every morning he could see

An angel walking on the sky;

Across the sunny skies of morn

He threw great handfuls far and nigh

Of poppy seed among the corn;

And then, he said, the angels run

To see the poppies in the sun.

James Stephens

A clapper bridge at Eastleach.

WE HAVE laid up simples against forgetfulness,
　For we the nesting missel-thrush have seen
Brooding above the weaving watercress;
　We have gone by water-meadows fresh and green
Studded with kingcups and with cuckoo flowers,
　By hedges newly fledged with blackthorn foam,
And rested, weary with happy hours,
　And twilight by the kindled hearth of home.

Sonnet

(To Tanya - Fairford April 1926)

This was our spring, our lucky Eastertide,
　By willowed brooks, and from a western shire
We shared a Monday of undaunted pride
　Of him who sang the old, the hearts desire;
England we were, and yet of England own
　The budding bough, the song, the builded stone.

John Drinkwater

One of the group known as the Dymock poets, John Drinkwater was a most versatile man. Accomplished poet, playwright, essayist, anthologist, actor, theatre producer and director, all whilst being full time manager of the Birmingham Repertory Theatre.

A Summer corner of Sudeley Castle.

From Endymion (Book 1)

A THING OF
Beauty

A THING of beauty is a joy for ever:
  Its loveliness increases; it will never
Pass into nothingness; but still will keep
  A bower quiet for us, and a sleep
Full of sweet dreams, and health,
  and quiet breathing.

John Keats

Perhaps the most gifted and tragic of the Romantic Poets, Keats died of
tuberculosis in 1821 aged 25 years.

In the grounds of Colesbourne Park.

His wish was granted. He died in 1944 aged 22years.

Let Me Not See Old Age

LET ME not see old age: Let me not hear
    The proferred help, the mumbled sympathy,
The well-meant tactful sophistries that mock
    Pathetic husks who once were strong and free,
And in youth's fickle triumph laughed and sang,
    Loved, and were foolish; and at the close have seen
The fruits of folly garnered, and that love,
    Tamed and encaged, stale into grey routine.
Let me not see old age; I am content
    With my few crowded years; laughter and strength
And song have lit the beacon of my life.
    Let me not see it fade, but when the long
September shadows steal across the square,
    Grant me this wish; they may not find me there.

D.R. Geraint Jones

The church of St Mary at Lower Slaughter.

Much loved Forest of Dean poet and writer who died in 1981.

Singing in the Streets

I HAD almost forgotten the singing in the streets,
  Snow piled up by the houses, drifting
Underneath the door, into the warm room,
  Firelight, lamplight, the little lame cat
Dreaming in soft sleep on the hearth, mother dozing,
  Waiting for Christmas to come, the boys and me
Trudging over blanket fields waving lanterns to the sky
  I had almost forgotten the smell, the feel of it all,
The coming back home, with girls laughing like stars
  Their cheeks, holly berries, me kissing one,
Silent tongued, soberly, by the long church wall.

Leonard Clark

Early morning near Cowley.

IF EVER I saw blessing in the air
   I see it now in this still early day
Where lemon green the vaporous morning drips
   Wet sunlight on the powder of my eye.

Blown bubble film of blue, the sky wraps round
   Weeds of warm light whose every root and rod
Splutters the soapy green, and all the world
   Sweats with the bead of summer in it's bud.

If ever I heard blessing it is there
   Where birds in trees that shoals and shadows are
Splash with their hidden wings and drops of sound
   Break on my ears their crests of throbbing air.

Laurie Lee

Laurie Lee died aged 83yrs in Slad near Stroud, the village he immortalised in one of the best loved books of the 20th Century, Cider with Rosie.

Morning rain.

In the Rain

IN THE rain.

When I turn away, on its fine stalk

Twilight has fined to naught, the parsley flower

Figures, suspended still and ghostly white,

The past hovering as it revisits the light.

Edward Thomas

One of the Dymock Poets most famous for his elegant verse about the English countryside. He was 37yrs, married with two children when he enlisted in 1915. He was killed at the Battle of Arras, Easter 1917.

The lane at the top of Aggs Hill Cheltenham.

Famously bohemian American poet who died in 1950. First female winner of the Pulitzer Prize.

TIME *does not bring* RELIEF

TIME does not bring relief; you all have lied
    Who told me time would ease me of my pain!
    I miss him in the weeping of the rain;
I want him at the shrinking of the tide;
    The old snows melt from every mountain-side,
And last year's leaves are smoke in every lane;
But last year's bitter loving must remain

Heaped on my heart, and my old thoughts abide.
    There are a hundred places where I fear
To go-so with this memory they brim.
    And entering with relief some quiet place
Where never fell his foot or shone his face
    I say, "There is no memory of him here!"
And so stand stricken, so remembering him.

Edna St. Vincent Millay

The lonely twisted beech on Cleeve known to millions of racegoers.

the Walk

YOU DID not walk with me
   Of late to the hill-top tree
By the gated ways,
   As in earlier days;
You were weak and lame,
   So you never came,
And I went alone, and I did not mind,
   Not thinking of you as left behind.

I walked up there to-day
   Just in the former way:
Surveyed around
   The familiar ground
By myself again:
   What difference, then?
Only that underlying sense
   Of the look of a room on returning thence.

Thomas Hardy

One of the greatest of all English writers, Hardy took to poetry late in life and wrote much of it to express the grief he knew after the death of his wife.

The start of an affair at the Cotswold Wild Life Park.

A Birthday

MY HEART is like a singing bird
   Whose nest is in a watered shoot:
My heart is like an apple-tree
   Whose boughs are bent with thickset fruit;
My heart is like a rainbow shell
   That paddles in a halcyon sea;
My heart is gladder than all these
   Because my love is come to me.

Christina Rossetti

London born of Italian parents Christina Rosetti was the leading
female poet of the late 19th Century.

Dawn in Ryton Woods.

The least known of the Dymock Poets but the leading light and the driving force behind them.

RYTON FIRS

NOW I breathe you again, my woods of Ryton:

  Not only golden with your daffodil light

Lying in pools on the loose dusky ground

  Beneath the larches, tumbling in broad rivers

Down sloping grass under the cherry trees

  And birches, but among your branches clinging

A mist of that Farrara gold I first

  Loved in those easy hours you made so green.

Lascelles Abercrombie

Cromwell's Chair, Farmcote.

CROMWELL'S CHAIR

HAVE YOU ever sat in Cromwell's Chair
  And watched the evening die?
Fading in the western sky
  And ebbing from the downland fields;
Till all the greens and blues and browns
  That paint the valley floor
are drowned, in the darkling shrouds of eventide;
  And all is peace, all is still,
On Cromwell's forlorn hill...

John Ryde

There are two Cromwell legends attached to the Roman Camp on Beckbury Hill. One is that Thomas Cromwell, Henry VIII's enforcer, sat here and watched the destruction of the great Abbey of Hailes in the valley below. The other is that Richard Devereux, Oliver Cromwell's enforcer, rested his men here en route to relieve the Royalist siege of Gloucester. Confusingly both men bore the title Earl of Essex.

Sezincote.

From...

THE OPENING WORLD

WE'D DRIVE to Sunday lunch at Sezincote:
  First steps in learning how to be a guest,
First wood-smoke-scented luxury of life
  In the large ambience of a country house.
Heavy with hawthorn scent were Cotswold lanes,
  Golden the church towers standing in the sun,
And Gordon Russell with his arts and crafts,
  Somewhere beyond in Broadway. Down the drive,
Under the early yellow leaves of oaks;
  One lodge is Tudor, one in Indian style.
The bridge, the waterfall, the Temple Pool-
  And there they burst on us, the onion domes,
Chajjahs and chattris made of amber stone:
  'Home of the Oaks', exotic Sezincote!

John Betjeman

Largely spurned by the intelligensia but greatly loved by the public
John Betjeman was not only Poet Laureate but a National Treasure. Had it
been possible I think he would have been the subject of a Preservation Order.

A view of Painswick from a Sheepscombe meadow.

Popular Stroud poet. One of several keeping the tradition of Gloucestershire poetry alive and well.

JUNE EVENING, STROUD VALLEY.

EVENING light slants over the valley
    swallows balance and skim;
their forked tails flick
    and the pale bellies gleam
like fish in a stream.

Trees lay down long shadows
    on meadows shaven and pale;
against dark clouds
    white dove wings shiver
like flowers in the river.

A shoulder of hill stands dark
    above the clustering town;
the thin spire catches light
    and it's gold bird glitters
like a jewel in the waters.

Sheila Simmons

Fleur Loney of Bristol with her Mother.

PATIENT GRISSIL

(Act IV, Scene II)

GOLDEN slumbers kisse your eyes,
Smiles awake you when you rise:
Sleepe pretty wantons doe not cry,
And I will sing a lullabie,
Rocke them rocke them lullabie.

Thomas Dekker

Prolific Elizabethan playwright, whose works have not weathered as well as some of his contemporaries. These lines were adapted and used by The Beatles on side two of Abbey Road.

Joan Barber of Cheltenham.

WHEN YOU ARE OLD

WHEN *you are old and grey and full of sleep,*
And nodding by the fire, take down this book,
And slowly read, and dream of the soft look
Your eyes had once, and of their shadows deep;

How many loved your moments of glad grace,
And loved your beauty with love false or true,
But one man loved the pilgrim soul in you,
And loved the sorrows of your changing face;

And bending down beside the glowing bars,
Murmur, a little sadly, how Love fled
And paced upon the mountains overhead
And hid his face amid a crowd of stars.

W.B.Yeats

William Butler Yeats. Inspirational Irish poet, artist, playwright, Nobel Prize winner and founder of the Abbey Theatre.

An orchard near May Hill.

Laurie Lee died aged 83yrs in Slad, the village he immortalised in one of the best loved books of the 20th Century, Cider with Rosie.

Apples

BEHOLD the apples' rounded worlds;
  Juice green of July rain,
The black polestar of flowers, the rind
  Mapped with it's crimson stain.

The russet, crab and cottage red
  Burn to the sun's hot brass,
Then drop like sweat from every branch
  And bubble in the grass.

They lie as wanton as they fall,
  And where they fall and break,
The stallion clamps his crunching jaws,
  The starling stabs his beak.

Laurie Lee

GWR station at Winchcombe.

No Gloucestershire anthology would be complete without this famous poem. In an act of mindless vandalism British Rail demolished the station in 1969, hence the photograph of Winchcombe. Visitors from all over the world can still be found disconsolately wandering around the village of Adlestrop.

ADLESTROP

YES, I remember Adlestrop-
The name, because one afternoon
Of heat the express-train drew up there
Unwontedly. It was late June.

The steam hissed. Someone cleared his throat.
No one left and no one came
On the bare platform. What I saw
Was Adlestrop - only the name

And willows, willow-herb, and grass,
And meadowsweet, and haycocks dry,
No whit less still and lonely fair
Than the high cloudlets in the sky.

And for that minute a blackbird sang
Close by, and round him, mistier,
Farther and farther, all the birds
Of Oxfordshire and Gloucestershire.

Edward Thomas

May Day on May Hill. Surely only the English…!

Victorian playwright and poet who eloped with Elizabeth Barrett after a celebrated love affair.

Home thoughts from Abroad

OH, TO be in England
Now that April's there,
And whoever wakes in England
Sees, some morning, unaware,
That the lowest boughs and the brushwood sheaf
Round the elm-tree bole are in tiny leaf,
While the chaffinch sings on the orchard bough
In England - now!

Robert Browning

The village of Naunton.

London born of Italian parents Christina Rossetti was the leading female poet of the late 19th Century. After her death Elgar set these bleak words to music to become one of the most loved of all Christmas carols.

A CHRISTMAS CAROL

IN THE *bleak mid-winter*
Frosty wind made moan,
Earth stood hard as iron,
Water like a stone;
Snow had fallen, snow on snow,
Snow on snow,
In the bleak mid-winter
Long ago.

Christina Rossetti

Brood mares at pasture near Painswick.

Son of a poor bricklayer Juhasz was born in Bia in 1928 and became one of Hungary's greatest poets.

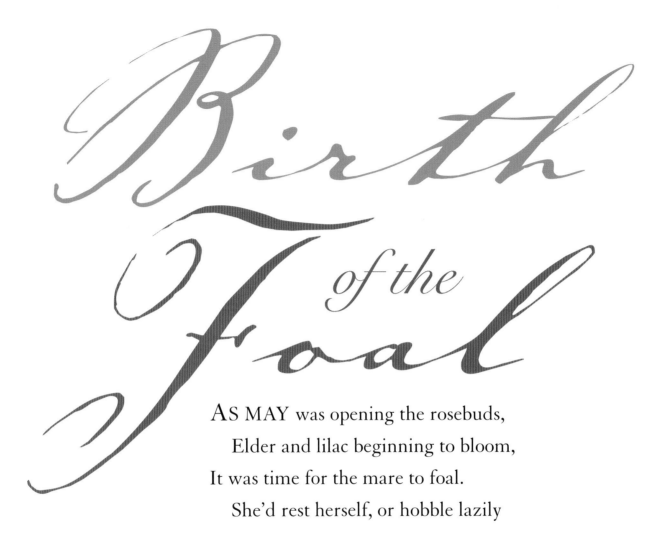

Birth of the Foal

AS MAY was opening the rosebuds,
  Elder and lilac beginning to bloom,
It was time for the mare to foal.
  She'd rest herself, or hobble lazily

After the boy who sang as he led her
  To pasture, wading through the meadow flowers.
They wandered back at dusk, bone-tired,
  The moon perched on a blue shoulder of sky.

Ferenc Juhasz

A pond at Frocester.

Ducks

FROM troubles of the world
    I turn to ducks,
Beautiful comical things
    Sleeping or curled
Their heads beneath white wings
    By water cool,
Or finding curious things
    To eat in various mucks
Beneath the pool,
    Tails uppermost, or waddling
Sailor-like on the shores
    Of ponds......

        F.W.Harvey

Will Harvey expressed his deep love of the County in wonderfully evocative poetry. He became known as the Gloucestershire Laureate.

Late summer in a Whittington garden.

The Red Admiral

THE WINGS tremble, it is the red admiral
    Ecstatically against the garden wall;
September is his enjoyment, but he does not know it,
    Name it or refer to it at all.

The old light fades upon the old stones;
    the day is old: how is there such light
From grey clouds? It is the autumnal equinox,
    And we shall all have shrunk before daylight.

C.H.Sisson

An Under Secretary in the Department of Employment it was not until his retirement that CHS became an outstanding poet.

The Romans brought edible snails to England and they have flourished in Chedworth woods ever since.

English poet who lived most of his life in America and died in 2004.

THE SNAIL pushes through a green
   Night, for the grass is heavy
With water and meets over
   The bright path he makes, where the rain
Has darkened the earth's dark. He
   Moves in a wood of desire,

Pale antlers barely stirring
   As he hunts. I cannot tell
What power is at work, drenched there
   With purpose, knowing nothing.
What is a snail's fury? All
   I think is that if later

I parted the blades above
   The tunnel and saw the thin
Trail of broken white across
   Litter, I would never have
Imagined the slow passion
   To that deliberate progress.

Thom Gunn

Considering the Snail

Cheltenham Races.

Prolific Ledbury poet and playwright and Poet Laureate for 37 years until his death in 1967.

An Epilogue

I HAVE seen flowers come in many stony places
And kind things done by men with ugly faces,
And the gold cup won by the worst horse at the races,
So I trust, too.

John Masefield

14th Century former monastic wool store in Bibury. One of the Cotswolds' most iconic views.

ARLINGTON ROW

A QUEUE of hungry infants, line astern for tea,
Higgledy piggledy, scruffily dressed,
An architect's nightmare, no less;
No neatness or straightness, no vision, no scale,
But look at the picture, look at the whole;
There is heart here, and character,
Beauty and soul.

John Ryde

I have no words that can do justice to Tintern Abbey. Visit it on a cold grey day, or in the early morning before the sun has cleared Offa's Dyke.

From
Childe Harold's
Pilgrimage

LOOK ON *its broken arch, its ruined wall,*
 Its chambers desolate, and portals foul:
Yes, this was once Ambition's airy hall,
 The dome of Thought, the palace of the Soul;
Behold through each lack-lustre, eyeless hole,
 The gay recess of Wisdom and of Wit
And Passion's host, that never brook'd control:
 Can all, saint, sage or sophist ever writ,
People this lonely tower, this tenement refit?

George Gordon, Lord Byron

No visit to the Cotswolds can be complete without a stop at Chipping Campden.

Chipping Camden

MY LADY Campden's subtleties
    Of honey stone and cool dark lanes.
Guards of honour, line abreast,
    Of gabled walls and stately halls,
Of cosy rose clad cottages
    With bonnets made of thatch.

John Ryde

Sunrise near Tetbury.

Perhaps the most gifted and tragic of the Romantic Poets, Keats died of tuberculosis in 1821 aged 25 years.

from
...TO AUTUMN

SEASON of mists and mellow fruitfulness!
Close bosom-friend of the maturing sun;

John Keats

Hartpury Mill.

Will Harvey was born at Murrel's End in the village of Hartpury in 1888.

After Long Wandering

I WILL go back to Gloucestershire,
    To the spot where I was born,
To the talk at eve with men and women
    And songs on the roads at morn.
And I'll sing as I tramp by dusty hedges
    Or drink my ale in the shade
How Gloucestershire is the finest home
    That the Lord God ever made.

F.W.Harvey

An obliging trio posing by the Windrush.

The Cow

THE COW is of the bovine ilk;
One end moo, the other, milk.

Ogden Nash

Humorous American poet who died in 1971.

Gloucester Old Spot piglets at Butt's Farm Cirencester.

The Pig

THE PIG, if I am not mistaken,
  Supplies us sausage, ham, and bacon.
Let others say his heart is big -
  I call it stupid of the pig.

Ogden Nash

A dead tree near Winchcombe that reminded Sally of the Jabberwock.

'TWAS brillig, and the slithy toves
　　Did gyre and gimble in the wabe:
All mimsey were the borogroves,
　　And the mome raths outgrabe.

Jabberwocky

'Beware the Jabberwock, my son!
　　The jaws that bite, the claws that catch!
Beware the Jubjub bird, and shun
　　The frumious Bandersnatch!'

And, as in uffish thought he stood,
　　The Jabberwock, with eyes of flame,
Came whiffling through the tulgey wood,
　　And burbled as it came!

Lewis Carroll

Writer of Alice in Wonderland. Alice lived for several years in
Charlton Kings and LC was a frequent visitor.

A sleepy morning on the banks of the Evenlode.

Leisure

WHAT life is this if, full of care,
  We have no time to stand and stare?-

No time to stand beneath the boughs,
  And stare as long as sheep and cows:

W.H.Davies

Welsh poet who spent much of his early life as a tramp in America and England. He rose to become one of the most popular poets of his day. He settled in Nailsworth where he died in 1940.

David Powell and his grandson Will walking in Pittville Park Cheltenham.

French born Belloc became a British citizen in his thirties and in 1906 was elected Liberal MP for South Salford.

Discovery

LIFE IS a long discovery, isn't it?

    You only get your wisdom bit by bit.

If you have luck you find in early youth

    How dangerous it is to tell the Truth;

And next you learn how dignity and peace

    Are the ripe fruits of patient avarice.

You find that middle life goes racing past.

    You find despair: and, at the very last,

You find as you are giving up the ghost

    That those who loved you best despised you most.

Hilaire Belloc

The exquisite face of the wild pansy said to mend a broken heart.

Radical poet from Warwick. He was rusticated from Oxford for firing a gun at a Tory. He inherited a fortune but spent a lot of it on leading his own private army to Spain to fight Napoleon. He somehow survived his turbulent life until he was 89yrs.

Heart's-Ease

THERE IS a flower I wish to wear,
But not until first worn by you…
Heart's-ease…of all earth's flowers most rare;
Bring it; and bring enough for two.

Walter Savage Landor

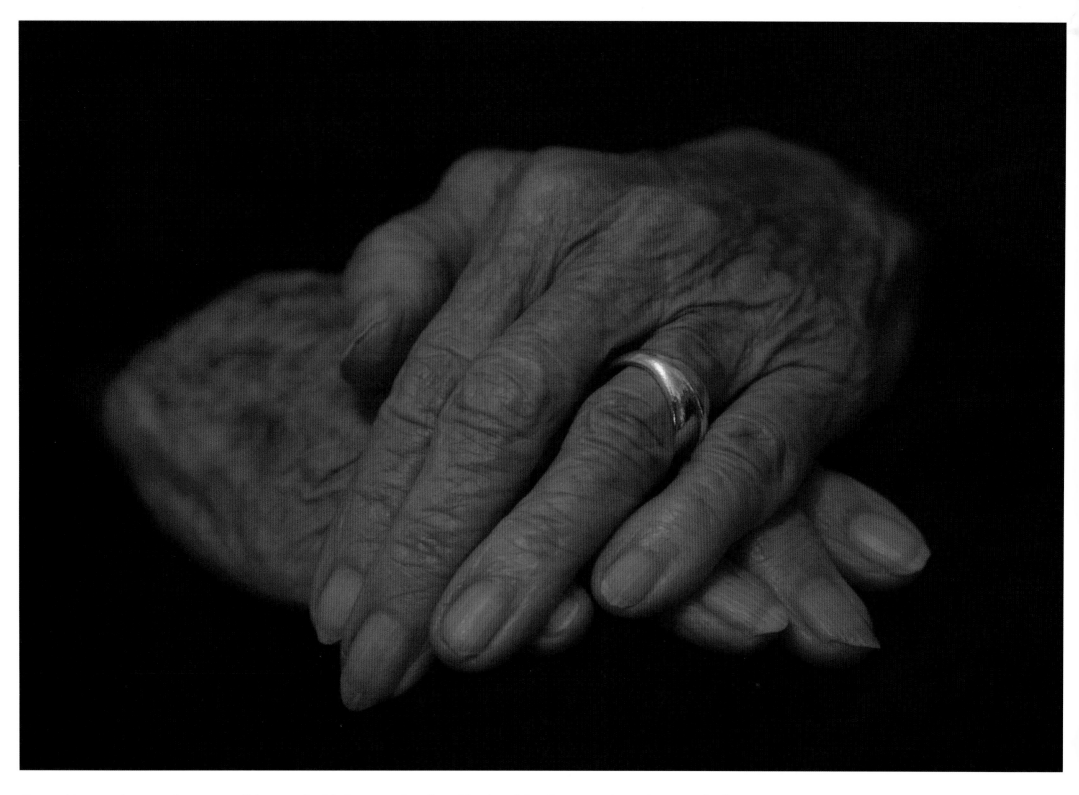

Cotswold poet who was almost as well known for his fearsome bowling. He played for Sheepscombe and once took all ten Barnsley wickets for eight runs. Laurie Lee described his fast one as "like a shot from a cannon."

SEE THESE HANDS

SEE these hands folded now,
  Hands that wrought for so many,
Tended and tidied a family,
  Soothed them and calmed them,
Fed, clothed and reared them
  Almost on nothing.

See these hands resting,
  That in the old hard days
Picked blackberries for pennies
  And gathered dry sticks in bundles,
In dim March days I scarcely remember
  When beech woods were a mystery
And fox cubs played among daffodils.

See these hands resting,
  That raked hay in the fields
Of a summer coloured with butterflies,
  That brought tea and sandwiches
To tired men at harvest,
  And scattered wheat and Argentinian maize
To hungry hens.

Frank Mansell

Leckhampton Hill.

Will Harvey expressed his deep love of the County in wonderfully evocative poetry, much of it written in the trenches. He became known as the Gloucestershire Laureate.

In Flanders

I'M HOMESICK for my hills again-
   My hills again!
To see above the Severn plain
   Unscabbarded against the sky
The blue high blade of Cotswold lie;

F.W.Harvey

Oxford Wagons at Bromesberrow.

The foremost English poet of the early eighteenth century. He converted a Twickenham cottage into a Palladian villa.
We only have contemporary accounts of the wonderful gardens and grottos he created on the banks of the Thames.

ODE *on* SOLITUDE

HAPPY the man, whose wish and care
  A few paternal acres bound,
Content to breathe his native air
  In his own ground.

Whose herds with milk, whose fields with bread,
  Whose flocks supply him with attire,
Whose trees in summer yield him shade,
  In winter fire.

Blest, who can unconcernedly find
  Hours, days, and years slide soft away,
In health of body, peace of mind,
  Quiet by day.

Thus let me live, unseen, unknown,
  Thus unlamented let me die,
Steal from the world, and not a stone
  Tell where I lie.

Alexander Pope

Duke and Emily begin their day's work near Newent.

Prolific Ledbury poet and playwright and Poet Laureate for 37 years until his death in 1967.

Autumn Ploughing

AFTER the ranks of stubble have lain bare,
    And field mice and the finches' beaks have found
The last spilled seed corn left upon the ground;
    And no more swallows miracle in air;

When the green tuft no longer hides the hare,
    And dropping starling flights at evening come;
When birds, except the robin, have gone dumb,
    And leaves are rustling downwards everywhere;

Then out, with the great horses, come the ploughs,
    And all day long the slow procession goes,
Darkening the stubble fields with broadening strips.

Gray sea-gulls settle after to carouse:
    Harvest prepares upon the harvest's close,
Before the blackbird pecks the scarlet hips.

John Masefield

The River Eye.

18th Century Scottish poet famous for composing the words to Rule Britannia. (SNP please note!)

FROM... WINTER

THE *cherish'd fields*

Put on their winter-robe of purest white.

'Tis brightness all; save where the new snow melts

Along the mazy current. Low the woods

Bow their hoar head; and, ere, the languid sun

Faint from the west emits his evening ray,

Earth's universal face, deep-hid and chill,

Is one wild dazzling waste, that buries wide

The works of man.

James Thomson

Walking in the Woods near Tetbury.

American poet, winner of the Pulitzer Prize on four occasions. He first found fame in England whilst one of the Dymock poets.

The Road Not Taken

TWO roads diverged in a yellow wood,
 And sorry I could not travel both
And be one traveller, long I stood
 And looked down one as far as I could
To where it bent in the undergrowth;

Then took the other, as just as fair,
 And having perhaps the better claim,
Because it was grassy and wanted wear;
 Though as for that the passing there
Had worn them really about the same,

And both that morning equally lay
 In leaves no step had trodden black.
Oh, I kept the first for another day!
 Yet knowing how way leads on to way,
I doubted if I should ever come back.

I shall be telling this with a sigh
 Somewhere ages and ages hence:
Two roads diverged in a wood, and I -
 I took the one less travelled by,
And that has made all the difference.

Robert Frost

Crickley Hill from Birdlip.

On Birdlip

I'VE TRAMPED a score of miles today
And now on Cotswold stand
Wondering if in any way
Their owners understand
How all those little gold fields I see
And the great green woods beyond
Have given themselves to me, to me
Who own not an inch of land.

FW Harvey

Kim Muir's grave on the heights of Cleeve. He is still commemorated by a steeplechase at the Cheltenham Festival.

The finance department of the Board of Trade cannot be the most fertile of soils to nurture the arts, but whilst rising from junior clerk to assistant secretary, Monkhouse became a leading Victorian poet and art critic.

Any Soul to any Body

SO WE must part, my body, you and I
    Who've spent so many pleasant years together.
'Tis sorry work to lose your company
    Who clove to me so close, whate'er the weather,
From winter unto winter, wet or dry;
    But I must journey on my way alone,
And leave you quietly beneath a stone.

But you must stay, dear body, and I go.
    And I was once so very proud of you:
You made my mother's eyes to overflow
    When first she saw you, wonderful and new.
And now, with all your faults, 'twere hard to find
    A slave more willing or a friend more true.
Ay-even they who say the worst about you
    Can scarcely tell what I shall do without you.

Cosmo Monkhouse

Snowshill Lavender Fields.

17th Century English folk song.

Lavender Blue

LAVENDERS' Blue, dilly dilly,
Lavenders' Green
When I am King, dilly dilly,
You will be Queen.

Anon

A quiet corner of the graveyard at the Church of St Lawrence.

One of the major English Romantic poets whose influence remains as strong now as ever. He drowned aged 29yrs while sailing in the Mediterranean

A Summer Evening
CHURCHYARD

Lechlade, Gloucestershire

THE wind has swept from the wide atmosphere
　　Each vapour that obscured the sunset's ray,
And pallid evening twines its beaming hair
　　In duskier braids around the languid eyes of day
Silence and twilight, unbeloved of men,
　　Creep hand in hand from yon obscurest glen....

...The dead are sleeping in their sepulchres:
　　And, mouldering as they sleep, a thrilling sound,
Half sense half thought, among the darkness stirs,
　　Breathed from their wormy beds all living things around,
And, mingling with the still night and mute sky,
　　Its awful hush is felt inaudibly.

Percy Bysshe Shelley

An angry sky over Cleeve.

The Cloud

I BRING fresh showers for the thirsting flowers,
  From the sea and the streams;
I bear light shade for the leaves when laid
  In their noonday dreams.
From my wings are shaken the dews that waken
  The sweet buds every one,
When rocked to rest on their mother's breast,
  As she dances about the sun.
I wield the flail of the lashing hail,
  And whiten the green plains under,
And then again I dissolve into rain,
  And laugh as I pass in thunder…

Percy Bysshe Shelley

The old Winchcombe road by Belas Knap.

Regarded by some as the greatest writer of the 20th Century GKC was a physical as well as a literary giant. He was also famously absent minded. He once sent a telegram to his wife saying "Am at Market Harborough, where should I be?"

The Rolling English Road

BEFORE the Roman came to Rye or out to Severn strode,
  The rolling English drunkard made the rolling English road.
A reeling road, a rolling road, that rambles round the shire,
  And after him the parson ran, the sexton and the squire;
A merry road, a mazy road, and such as we did tread
  The night we went to Birmingham by way of Beachy Head.

Gilbert Keith Chesterton

A misty morning in Leighterton.

Popular Forest poet who died in 2007.

From...
Autumn
Swan Song

THE stealthy, creeping mists enshroud the countryside

   Erasing scenery, like soft grey curtains drawn across a lighted window.

And Autumn - having nearly played her part,

   Picks up her ragged skirts for one more bow

While Winter waits and watches in the wings.

Joyce Latham

The Church of St Lawrence looking over Moreton and the Fosse Way.

Poet Laureate whose straightforward and at times simple verse found little favour among intellectuals but was greatly loved by the people at large.

FROM... *the Opening World*

...AT SIX o'clock from Bourton-on-the-Hill
The bells rang out above the clumps of oak;
A lighter peal from Longborough lingered on;
Moreton-in-Marsh came echoing from the vale...
So gently broke the triple waves of sound
On a still evening of enormous light
That, when they ceased, I almost seemed to hear
From open church-doors village voluntaries
A mile and more away.

John Betjeman

Autumn at Westonbirt.

Killed on the Somme in 1916 Cheltenham Poet Winterbotham left us only fragments of beautiful and poignant verse.

From ...Autumn

WHAT have we now when the east winds are
Whirling the ruin of Summer to earth?
The blossoms of Spring-time are dead, but in dying
Gave all the fruits of the Autumn their birth.

Cyril Winterbotham

A Kitchen Garden near Cirencester.

Writer, poet and chronicler of the Empire.

The Glory of the Garden

OUR England is full of stately views,
    Of borders, beds and shrubberies and lawns and avenues,
With statues on the terraces and peacocks strutting by;
    But the Glory of the Garden lies in more than meets the eye.

For where the old thick laurel grow, along the thin red wall,
    You find the tool-and potting-sheds which are the heart of all;
The cold-frames and the hot-houses, the dung pits and the tanks,
    The rollers, carts and drain-pipes, with the barrows and the planks.

Rudyard Kipling

Beech in the Forest of Dean.

The Wood

THERE was a wood of beech trees near my home
 Whose roots were twisted round the pitted rocks,
And in the branches every spring
 The thrushes sang so constantly
The glens became a single chord of sound.
 The sun lay all along the faces of the leaves
And on the swinging rows of scentless flowers;
 The wood stretched far into the silences,
But as you leaped from rock to rock, you heard
 The tiny notes of water dripping on the bright stones
And orchestras of insects underground,
 You saw the ferns uncurling baby fronds
And sudden islands of forget-me-nots…

…And when at last you reached the circling wire

   That cut in two this trembling forest world,

You plunged into a hundred seas of bluebell light

   And like a crazy traveller drugged and lost

In undiscovered continents,

   You sank, defeated, drenched with flowers,

Beneath the drowning tides that wandered there.

Leonard Clark

Much loved Forest of Dean poet and writer who died in 1981.

Bluebells in the Forest of Dean.

Summer on Salter's Hill.

Friend of the Rossettis and the Pre Raphaelites, by the time he was 30 Swinburne had become England's foremost poet.

The Garden of Proserpine

HERE, where the world is quiet;
Here, where all trouble seems
Dead winds' and spent waves' riot
In doubtful dreams of dreams;
I watch the green field growing
For reaping folk and sowing,
For harvest-time and mowing,
A sleepy world of streams.

Algernon Charles Swinburne

Of all the blossoms at Westonbirt the Cherry reigns supreme.

Severe reticent and remote classical scholar, poetry to Housman was a secondary activity. He still managed to compile A Shropshire Lad, one of England's most enduring collections. "Do you know the poems of Professor Housman" asked Rupert Brooke. "No I supposed not."

LOVELIEST of trees, the cherry now
   Is hung with bloom along the bough,
And stands about the woodland ride
   Wearing white for Eastertide.

Now, of my threescore years and ten,
   Twenty will not come again,
And take from seventy springs a score,
   It only leaves me fifty more.

And since to look at things in bloom
   Fifty springs are little room,
About the woodlands I will go
   To see the cherry hung with snow.

Alfred Edward Housman

The Evenlode at Ascott under Wychwood.

From DEDICATORY ODE

THE quiet evening kept her tryst:
  Beneath an open sky we rode
And passed into a wandering mist
  Along the perfect Evenlode.

The tender Evenlode that makes
  Her meadows hush to hear the sound
Of waters mingling in the brakes,
  And binds my heart to English ground.

A lovely river, all alone,
  She lingers in the hills and holds
A hundred little towns of stone,
  Forgotten in the western wolds.

Hilaire Belloc

French born Belloc became a British citizen in his thirties and in 1906 was elected Liberal MP for South Salford.

The Wye. Queen of British Rivers.

LINES COMPOSED A FEW MILES ABOVE TINTERN ABBEY, ON REVISITING THE BANKS OF THE WYE DURING A TOUR

JULY 13, 1798

FIVE years have past; five summers, with the length
Of five long winters! And again I hear
These waters, rolling from their mountain-springs
With a soft inland murmur. -Once again
Do I behold these steep and lofty cliffs,
That on a wild secluded scene impress
Thoughts of more deep seclusion; and connect
The landscape with the quiet of the sky.

William Wordsworth

Founder, with Coleridge, of the Romantic Movement, Poet Laureate, and one of England's major poets.

Winget Seconds versus Swindon CC at the Spa.

WG was the most famous Gloucestershire cricketer of them all. He was a belligerent man. He once played in a charity match which attracted a very large crowd. He was given out first ball but refused to walk. When the umpire kept his finger aloft, WG pointedly looked around at the multitude, then roared "They've come to see me bat man, not you umpire."

GRACE *at* GLOUCESTER

I SAW the 'Old Man' once
    When he was old as I
Was young. He did not score,
    So far as I recall, a heap of runs,
Nor even hit a four.
    But still he lives before my schoolboy eye
A giant among pygmies. In his hand
    The bat looked like a toy. I saw him stand
Firm set on legs as massive as the piers
    Of the Norman nave at Gloucester; and the cheers
Which greeted him on the 'Spa' were heard
    As far as the Cathedral. When he stirred
The ground shook, and the crazy old
    Pavilion creaked and groaned.
I saw him field at point

When 'Father' Roberts bowled
    And the batsman, now forgotten, from the group
Around the wicket cut a fast one square
    Along the ground, the Doctor saw it there
A moment ere it was concealed
    By his great bulk. He did not deign to stoop,
But let it pass. He bowled a few
    Himself, slow lumbering to the crease.
The batsmen knew
    By then his simple bluff, and did not care.

Upon the Spa no county players pace;
    The great ones of to-day it does not know.
I deem it better so,
    Leaving the elm-grit field its dream of Grace.

Oscar Lloyd

Cranham Woods.

The tortured genius that was Ivor Gurney survived the First World War but returned suffering from shell shock.
They locked him away in a mental institution for the rest of his life.

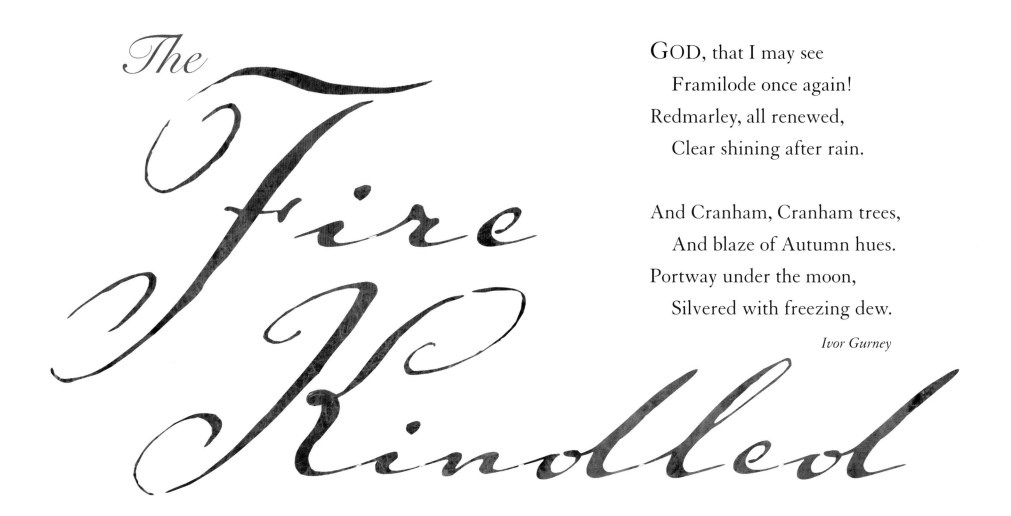

The Fire Kindled

GOD, that I may see
    Framilode once again!
Redmarley, all renewed,
    Clear shining after rain.

And Cranham, Cranham trees,
    And blaze of Autumn hues.
Portway under the moon,
    Silvered with freezing dew.

Ivor Gurney

A Winchcombe garden in it's summer dress.

Sonnet XVIII

SHALL I compare thee to a summer's day?
Thou art more lovely and more temperate:
Rough winds do shake the darling buds of May,
And summer's lease hath all too short a date:

William Shakespeare

Copse Hill near Stow.

One of the 20th Century's great poets who had to bear the cross of having written Lady Chatterley's Lover.

A Winter's Tale

YESTERDAY the fields were only grey with scattered snow,
  And now the longest grass leaves hardly emerge,
Yet her deep footsteps mark the snow, and go
  On towards the pines at the hill's white verge.

I cannot see her, since the mist's white scarf
  Obscures the dark wood and the dull orange sky;
But she's waiting, I know, impatient and cold, half
  Sobs struggling into her frosty sigh.

Why does she come so promptly, when she must know
  That she's only the nearer to the inevitable farewell;
The hill is steep, on the snow my steps are slow-
  Why does she come, when she knows what I have to tell?

DH Lawrence

In the grounds of Woodchester Mansion.

Rain

NOTHING but the wild rain
   On this bleak hut, and solitude, and me
Remembering again that I shall die
   And neither hear the rain nor give it thanks
For washing me cleaner than I have been
   Since I was born into this solitude.

Edward Thomas

Abbotswood.

Streams

(FOR ELIZABETH DREW)

DEAR water, clear water, playful in all your streams,
    As you dash or loiter through life who does not love
To sit beside you, to hear you and see you,
    pure being, perfect in music and movement?

W.H.Auden

One of the 20th Century's most controversial and influential poets.

A meadow above Guiting Power.

Although a member of the House of Lords, Byron was a radical. He supported the Luddites and was an impassioned advocate of social reform. He fought in Italy's war with Austria and then joined the Greek rebellion against their Turkish rulers. He died from fever in Missolonghi.

From
Childe Harold's
Pilgrimage 4(3)

THE GREEN hills

   Are clothed with early blossoms, through the grass

The quick-eyed lizard rustles, and the bills

   Of summer-birds sing welcome as ye pass;

Flowers fresh in hue, and many in their class,

   Implore the pausing step, and with their dyes

Dance in the soft breeze in a fairy mass;

   The sweetness of the violet's deep blue eyes,

Kissed by the breath of heaven, seems coloured by its skies.

George Gordon, Lord Byron

The lane to Alderton.

To Ivor Gurney

NOW hawthorn hedges live again;
And all along the banks below
Pale primrose fires have lit the lane
Where oft we wandered long ago
And saw the blossom blow.

F.W.Harvey

Part of the glorious ruins at Sudeley.

University Lecturer, jazz musician and determined Midlander, Roy Fisher is one of England's leading living poets.

From By the POND

IT DRAWS light to itself, especially at sunset, standing still and smooth faced, looking westwards at the hill. I am not able to imagine the activity that must once have been here. I can see no ghosts of men and women, only the gigantic ghost of stone. They are too frightened of it to pull it down.

Roy Fisher

The graveyard of the Church of St Peter, Leckhampton.

Younger brother of Dame Edith.

FROM *England* RECLAIMED

SOUND out, proud trumpets,
    And you, bugles, blow
        Over the English Dead,
Not slain in battle, in no sense sublime.
These rustic figures caught at last by Time,
And yet their blood was warm and red
As any roses that in England grow.
To these anonymous armies of the Dead
    Blow, bugles, blow;

Sound out, proud trumpets, let your brazen thunder
Wake them, to make them pass
Before us under the wide sky.
Thunder, drums and trumpets, thunder,
Wake them, to rise from where they lie
Under
    Under
        Under
            The green grass
        Under the wide grey sky.

Osbert Sitwell

The COMBE

A combe by the lane to Ford.

THE *Combe was ever dark, ancient and dark.*

   Its mouth is stopped with bramble, thorn and briar;

And no one scrambles over the sliding chalk

   By beech and yew and perishing juniper

Down the half precipices of its sides, with roots

   And rabbit holes for steps. The sun of Winter,

The moon of Summer, and all the singing birds

   Except the missel-thrush that loves the juniper,

Are quite shut out. But far more ancient and dark

   The Combe looks since they killed the badger there,

Dug him out and gave him to the hounds,

   That most ancient Briton of English beasts.

Edward Thomas

One of the Dymock Poets most famous for his elegant verse about the English countryside. He was 37yrs, married with two children when he enlisted in 1915. He was killed at the Battle of Arras, Easter 1917.

The Corner Cupboard at Winchcombe.

A GLASS *of* BEER

THE lanky hank of a she in the inn over there
    Nearly killed me for asking the loan of a glass of beer;
May the devil grip the whey-faced slut by the hair,
    And beat bad manners out of her skin for a year.

If I asked her master he'd give me a cask a day;
    But she, with the beer at hand, not a gill would arrange!
May she marry a ghost and bear him a kitten, and may
    The High King of Glory permit her to get the mange.

James Stephens

James Stephens was born in Dublin in 1882. It must be very difficult to become a great Irish Poet, there is so much competition, but his voice was unique.

The haul from a long afternoon on Dixton Hill.

Irish poet who was awarded the Nobel prize for literature in 1995.

Blackberry Picking

LATE august, given heavy rain and sun

    For a full week, the blackberries would ripen.

At first, just one, a glossy purple clot

    Among others, red, green, hard as a knot.

You ate that first one and its flesh was sweet

    Like thickened wine: summer's blood was in it

Leaving stains upon the tongue and lust for

    Picking. The red ones inked up and that hunger

Sent us out with milk-cans, pea-tins, jam-pots

    Where briars scratched and wet grass bleached our boots.

Seamus Heaney

The monument, on Nibley Knoll is to William Tyndale, translator of the Bible. Three miles across the valley, 250 years later another man who changed the world was born. Dr Edward Jenner.

Born in 1819 Walt Whitman was to become the greatest of all American poets. A personal view of course but one shared by many.

From... LEAVES *of* GRASS

STOP this day and night with me and you shall possess the origin of all poems,
  You shall possess the good of the earth and sun....there are millions of suns left,
You shall no longer take things at second or third hand....nor look through the
  eyes of the dead....nor feed on the spectres in books,
You shall not look through my eyes either, nor take things from me,
  You shall listen to all sides and filter them from yourself.

I have heard what the talkers were talking....the talk of the beginning and the end,
  But I do not talk of the beginning or the end.

Walt Whitman

Acknowledgements

Our grateful thanks to the following for permission to use copyright material.

David Higham Associates for England Reclaimed by Osbert Sitwell, Faber and Faber Ltd for Considering the Snail by Thom Gunn, PFD Ltd (www.PFD.co.uk) April Rise and Apples by Laurie Lee and for Dedicatory Ode and Discovery by Hilaire Belloc (Copyright © the Estate of Hilaire Belloc) A.P.Watt Ltd on behalf of Grainne Yeats, Executrix of the Estate of Michael Butler Yeats for When You are Old by William Butler Yeats, John Murray (Publishers) Ltd for The Opening World by John Betjeman, Bloodaxe Books Ltd (www.bloodaxebooks.com) for The Long and the Short of it: Poems 1955 - 2005 by Roy Fisher, The Society of Authors as the Literary Representative of the Estate of James Stephens for In the Poppy Field and A Glass of Beer, the Authors' Licensing and Collecting Society.

We have made every effort to contact all copyright holders or their heirs, but in some cases have been unsuccessful.
All such copyright holders are invited to contact the publishers if they wish.

We are also indebted to:

John McKenna, David and Will Powell, Cotswold Wildlife Park, Joan Barber, Helen Loney, Tom Rucker, Cheltenham Plant Centre, Gavin and Carol Hughes-Jones, Gina Bore, Tom Ryde, David Williams, Adrian and Jo Eastman, Edward Gillespie, Cotswold Farm Park, Butt's Farm, Michael and Elizabeth Vaquer, Elizabeth Billot and Peter Baitup.